*Catch on fire with
enthusiasm and people
will come for miles to
watch you burn.*

John Wesley

101 ways to find God's purpose for your life

Natalie Gillespie

Creative Edge

101 Ways to Find God's Purpose for Your Life
ISBN: 1-40378-072-2

Published in 2006 by Creative Edge, an imprint of Dalmatian Press, LLC.
Copyright © 2006 Dalmatian Press, LLC. Franklin, Tennessee 37067.

Editor: Lila Empson
Cover and Text Design: Whisner Design Group

08 09 CLI 10 9 8 7 6 5 4 3

Printed in the U.S.A.

CE10296

*If you begin to
live life looking
for the God that is
all around you,
every moment
becomes a prayer.*

Frank Bianco

Contents

Introduction
Discover Your Strengths . . . .#1
Uncover the Joy of You . . . .#2
Rest in God . . . .#3
Try Something New . . . .#4
Pray for Direction . . . .#5
Refine Your Talents . . . .#6
Meditate on God's Word . . . .#7
Exercise Your Body . . . .#8
Examine Your Emotions . . . .#9
Engage Your Spirit . . . .#10
Listen to Loved Ones . . . .#11
Know Your Worth . . . .#12
Practice Lots of Loving . . . .#13
Take Time for God . . . .#14
Fellowship with Friends . . . .#15
Embrace Each Day . . . .#16
Enjoy What You Have . . . .#17
Test Yourself . . . .#18
Expect the Difficulties . . . .#19
Find Strength in Numbers . . . .#20
Make a Difference . . . .#21
Visit the Past . . . .#22
Set God-Given Goals . . . .#23
Give Graciously . . . .#24

Consider the Children . . . . #25
Educate Yourself . . . . #26
Give God Your Best . . . . #27
Sing a New Song . . . . #28
Lean on Him . . . . #29
Observe Creation . . . . #30
Learn from Mistakes . . . . #31
Enter into Worship . . . . #32
Look Up, Not Down . . . . #33
Become a Seed Planter . . . . #34
Take Good Advice . . . . #35
Get Away with God . . . . #36
Read Great Works . . . . #37
Let Go of Grudges . . . . #38
Set the Example . . . . #39
Remember His Story . . . . #40
Celebrate His Life . . . . #41
Determine Your Gifts . . . . #42
Listen Carefully . . . . #43
Laugh Out Loud . . . . #44
Learn About Heaven . . . . #45
Seek Ye First . . . . #46
Take a Break . . . . #47
Entertain Angels . . . . #48
Find a Church That Fits . . . . #49

Contents continued...

Celebrate Jesus' Birth . . . . #50
Stand Up Straight . . . . #51
Hand Over the Control . . . . #52
Smile a Lot . . . . #53
Ask the Hard Questions . . . . #54
Watch God Work . . . . #55
Teach Your Family . . . . #56
Be Willing to Move . . . . #57
Love the Unlovable . . . . #58
Go on a Retreat . . . . #59
Write Out Reminders . . . . #60
Read Through the Word . . . . #61
Don't Jump the Gun . . . . #62
Ask for Forgiveness . . . . #63
Take Communion . . . . #64
Work Diligently . . . . #65
Hand Out Compliments . . . . #66
Stand Still Sometimes . . . . #67
Learn "Love Languages" . . . . #68
Turn Off the Noise . . . . #69
Let Anger Out . . . . #70
Sacrifice Something . . . . #71
Play for a Day . . . . #72
Keep the Main Focus . . . . #73
Get Rid of Guilt . . . . #74
Reach Out to the Lost . . . . #75

Hold Your Head High . . . .#76
Know Your Neighbors . . . .#77
Prepare for Greatness . . . .#78
Grow Through Grief . . . .#79
Extend Grace and Mercy . . . .#80
Volunteer Your Skills . . . .#81
Memorize Scriptures . . . .#82
Take Deep Breaths . . . .#83
Smell a Flower . . . .#84
Encourage Others . . . .#85
Look Behind You . . . .#86
Wait Patiently . . . .#87
Bind Up Bitterness . . . .#88
Go Fishing . . . .#89
Watch Others Work . . . .#90
Stand in the Gap . . . .#91
Count Your Blessings . . . .#92
Pursue Passion . . . .#93
Resurrect Him Daily . . . .#94
Get on Your Knees . . . .#95
Run the Race . . . .#96
Ask for Answers . . . .#97
Let Him Have It . . . .#98
Create a New Habit . . . .#99
Face Forward . . . .#100
Start Right Now . . . .#101

Introduction

101 Ways to Find God's Purpose for Your Life
offers you valuable ways to connect with
God's unique plan for you. It will help you sort
through your daily activities, attitudes, and
actions and align them to fulfill God's special
purpose. You will learn that God created you
from a one-of-a-kind design and prepared
tasks for you to accomplish in ways that no
one else can. By examining the Bible, your
daily habits, and the practical ways you seek
God, *101 Ways to Find God's Purpose for
Your Life* will enhance your efforts by provid-
ing clarity and illumination, helping you grow
spiritually.

May *101 Ways to Find God's Purpose for
Your Life* deepen your connection with God,
invigorate your prayer life, and enrich your
relationship with him.

Dependence upon God makes heroes of ordinary people like you and me!

Bruce Wilkinson

I will be happy because of you; God Most High, I will sing praises to your name.

Psalm 9:2 NCV

#1

Discover Your Strengths

strengths

Think back to when you were a child. What were some of your favorite things to do? Did you care for injured animals, love to draw pictures, or delight in playing with friends? Now think of the ways those traits manifest themselves in your life today. Do you still collect "strays"—animals or people? Do you express yourself artistically through decorating and creating? Do you love to fix broken things? Do you enjoy opening your home to family and friends?

God's purpose for your life can be found in the passions and dreams he gave you. Use them to the fullest by devoting time and energies to the things you already love. Begin today.

> *We all have a calling. We all have a purpose in life. Not all of us are meant to be artists who paint on canvases, but we all have a gift. Sometimes it is presented to us early in our lives, and other times we realize our special gifts later, when we least expect.*
>
> **Mark Victor Hansen**

>> Make a list of your strengths, gifts, and talents. Write down the ways you are using your strengths in the tasks you perform daily.

#2

Uncover the Joy of You

> *Each one should use whatever gift he has received to serve others, faithfully administering God's grace in its various forms.*
>
> 1 Peter 4:10 NIV

joy

You are the only one who can do exactly what God has planned for you. The biblical Queen Esther was an orphan, and yet she was put in the right place at the right time to save a nation. Albert Einstein had behavioral problems, dyslexia, and was a poor speller, and yet he formulated the theory of relativity.

Value what God has given you. Creating home-cooked meals that are nutritious is a gift. Balancing roles of teacher, worker, parent, grandparent, spouse, and friend is a gift. Loving those around you is the ultimate gift. You have talents and abilities that are uniquely yours. Thank God for them.

>> Look at yourself in the mirror today without finding faults and flaws. Recognize your uniqueness, and notice the difference when you smile.

#3
Rest in God

In Hebrew, one definition of *rest* is "to be silent, be still, wait, be dumb, and grow dumb." Resting in God helps illuminate his purpose for your life because it requires no activity on your part. It demands silence, so that God can do his work in you.

To rest in him, you temporarily set aside the demands of the day in order to let God reveal himself to you. Taking time out in the midst of many demands on your time may not be easy, but it is necessary for the health of your mind, body, emotions, and spirit.

rest

> *Give God His glory by resting in Him, by trusting Him fully, by waiting patiently for Him.*
>
> Andrew Murray

≫ Build at least ten minutes of stillness and quiet into your day today to rest in him.

#4

Try Something New

He Who is seated on the throne said, See! I make all things new.

Revelation 21:5 AMP

new

As a child, do you remember the joy you felt when you tried something new and accomplished it for the first time? Whether it was something as simple as learning to snap your fingers or as complex as tying your shoe, the joy and satisfaction felt in first-time victories were unsurpassed.

Have you felt that thrill of discovery lately? Or have you packed your life full of the familiar and the routine? Trying something new like joining a scrapbooking club or playing racquetball can reenergize your life and reveal an aspect of God's unique purpose for you.

>> Add spice to your life by signing up for a class you've always wanted to take, learning to ballroom dance, or cooking a new dish.

#5

Pray for Direction

If a young whale were to lose its sense of direction, it might end up on the beach. If migrating flocks of birds were to lose their instinctive sense of direction, they might end up in Alaska instead of Florida, facing harsh conditions instead of basking in the sunny South. When people lose their sense of spiritual direction, they often reach a dead end in their jobs, their marriages, and their families.

How is your sense of direction? In order to uncover God's purpose for your life, you need to be headed in the right direction. Ask God to get your life pointed toward him.

pray

Nobody can know God unless God teaches him.

Saint Irenaeus

≫ Picture yourself navigating an unfamiliar city without maps or directions. Imagine hitting dead end after dead end. Thank God for the direction he gives you, and ask him to lead your way.

#6

Refine Your Talents

> *Let all the skilled craftsmen among you come and make everything that the LORD has commanded.*
>
> Exodus 35:10 HCSB

refine

God designed each human being with unique talents, gifts, and abilities that are meant to be developed for his glory. An undeveloped talent is like a fertilized field that never grows, a muscle that withers from atrophy, or a promise unfulfilled. An undeveloped talent is a waste.

If Michelangelo never studied his craft, there would be no breathtaking mural on the ceiling of the Sistine Chapel and no masterpiece like *David*. While you may not believe you have what it takes to craft a *David*, God has endowed you with talents and skills. Determine to practice and refine your abilities for him.

>> Pick up the guitar again, grab a paintbrush and a canvas, or use your singing skills. Take the talents you are using for God to the next level for his glory.

#7

Meditate on God's Word

Meditating means to go beyond mere thinking about it. Meditating implies centering thoughts around a concept, turning the concept over, and going back to it again and again.

Meditating on Scripture is a great way to find God's purpose, for it is in the Bible that he reveals his directives. When you meditate on the Bible, you gain spiritual maturity and wisdom. The Reverend Richard Baxter wrote in the seventeenth century that just as your digestive system processes the food you eat for your body to use, meditation digests the things of God and makes them a power that renews your heart.

meditate

> *Watch your thoughts; they become words. Watch your words; they become actions. Watch your actions; they become habits. Watch your habits; they become character. Watch your character; it becomes your destiny.*
>
> Author Unknown

>> Meditate on a favorite Bible verse, creed, or prayer by reflecting on the full meaning of *meditate*: "to contemplate or reflect, to focus your thoughts or ponder."

#8

Exercise Your Body

> *Physical exercise has some value, but spiritual exercise is much more important, for it promises a reward in both this life and the next.*
>
> 1 Timothy 4:8 NLT

exercise

Exercise provides many benefits to your life, and keeping in shape is part of God's purpose for you. Exercise keeps your body healthy and strong, your mind alert, and your emotions positive, releasing natural chemicals that stimulate good feelings. Sedentary bodies lead to minds that are unfocused, emotions that are out of control, and a spirit that wrestles with resting in him. Exercise helps develop a positive self-image.

God expects his followers to develop discipline—mentally, emotionally, spiritually, and physically—in order to unveil his best work in them.

≫ Begin the day with a brisk walk. Determine to implement a new exercise program; pat yourself on the back if you already exercise regularly, and keep up the good work.

#9

Examine Your Emotions

God's top priority for you is more about chasing holiness than pursuing happiness. God desires you to turn the focus from the way you feel to what you should do. Too often, people abandon good work that pleases God—a marriage, a career, a ministry—because they don't feel like doing it anymore. They don't *feel* like they are in love. They don't *feel* fulfilled.

If you tend to act hastily based on the way you feel, consider the ways your emotions influence your decision-making. Ask God to arrange your actions today according to his will rather than according to your feelings.

emotions

> *Many persons have a wrong idea of what constitutes true happiness. It is not attained through self-gratification but through fidelity to a worthy purpose.*
>
> **Helen Keller**

≫ Pray that God will give you strength to carry out his purpose in your life today, even if you don't feel like doing the tasks at hand.

#10

Engage Your Spirit

> *Create in me a clean heart, O God. Renew a right spirit within me.*
>
> Psalm 51:10 NLT

engage

Great people are often remembered because of their spirit, their determination to consume every drop of their cup of life, despite their circumstances. Teenager Anne Frank died because of Nazi oppression during World War II. She left behind a diary that touches people everywhere because of her indomitable spirit and optimism.

Helen Keller, although she could neither see nor hear, graduated from Radcliffe College, spoke around the world, and was awarded the Presidential Medal of Freedom by President Lyndon Johnson. Keller was determined to make the most of God's purpose for her life.

>> Wholeheartedly participate in life today. See things with spiritual eyesight as well as your physical eyes. Notice the beauty of creation, the glorious colors, smells, and sounds that surround you.

#11

Listen to Loved Ones

The older you get, the more you realize your parents are a lot smarter than you thought they were. People who love you—friends, parents, cousins, siblings—are on your side and usually want what is best for you.

God placed friends and family around you to help you discover his purpose for you. He gave you loved ones who know you and can give you a different perspective in difficult situations. Loved ones with different experiences and different opinions broaden your world and help you discover yourself. Allow them to speak wisdom into your life so that you can learn something new.

listen

> *Cherish your human connections: your relationships with friends and family.*
>
> Barbara Bush

≫ Write thank-you notes to loved ones today for their valuable input into your life.

#12

Know Your Worth

> *"Come, follow me,"*
> *Jesus said, "and*
> *I will make you*
> *fishers of men."*
>
> Mark 1:17 NIV

worth

You are infinitely valuable to God, so valuable that if you were the only person he created on Earth, he would still have sent Christ to die for you so that he could have an eternal relationship with you. Finding God's purpose for your life lies in reveling in how priceless you are to him and in seeing yourself through his eyes.

God made each human being an individual that he loves immensely and personally. He has called you for a special series of tasks that only you can perform. He follows your every movement, and he wants you to follow him.

≫ Draw a picture of yourself the way God sees you—as beautiful, royal, and priceless. Ask God to give you that picture of yourself.

#13

Practice Lots of Loving

Love is so important to God that it is mentioned hundreds of times in every translation of the Bible. Christ referred to love as the greatest commandment of all, and he spent his ministry demonstrating love to his followers.

Learning to love God's way provides the most tangible picture of him available to the world. Nothing will draw you closer to him or to others than walking in unconditional love. God-inspired love does not operate like a romance novel. True love encompasses enthusiasm and passion, and it bases itself more on trust, commitment, and action. It remains committed. Practice real love today.

love

> *To love is to will the good of another.*
>
> Saint Thomas Aquinas

≫ Love someone today through your actions: give a gift, a loving touch, a personal note, or an act of kindness.

#14

Take Time for God

> *Seven times a day I praise you for your righteous ordinances.*
>
> Psalm 119:164 NRSV

time

Relationships develop over time. Best friends become best friends because they invest lots of time in getting to know each other intimately. Good marriages sustain themselves because the lovers cement their bond by spending plenty of time together.

You can have a deep relationship with God and determine his purpose for your life by devoting time to the pursuit of a relationship with him. Setting aside time to get to know him through meditation on the Bible, praise of his attributes and goodness to you, study of Scripture, and conversation with him in prayer creates intimacy between you and the one who made you.

≫ Take out your calendar and schedule seven times of prayer, study, and praise today.

#15

Fellowship with Friends

As part of his purpose for your life, God created you to be in fellowship with other people. While it is perfectly acceptable to spend time alone, it is equally important to develop and nurture deep friendships. Friendships add accountability as well as joy to your life. True friends help shoulder sorrows, bear burdens, and express excitement.

Life can become so filled with work, spouse, children, errands, and chores that taking time to fellowship with friends may rank low on the list of priorities. Fellowship needs to rank near the top so that friends and family can share your excitement and pain.

friends

> *My best friend is the one who brings out the best in me.*
>
> Henry Ford

≫ Push unimportant interferences out of your day, and schedule time to meet with a close friend as soon as you can. While you're at it, write or e-mail an old friend and renew your relationship.

dream

101 ways to

value

rest

discover

uncover

find God's purpose for your life

practice

meditate

exercise

#16

Embrace Each Day

> They ate and drank
> with great joy in
> the presence of the
> LORD that day.
>
> 1 Chronicles 29:22
> NIV

embrace

You can always find God's purpose for you by making the most of each day that he gives you. Yesterday is gone and will never return. The lessons learned from yesterday are important to keep in mind, but you can't live there. Plans for tomorrow are great, but tomorrow may never come.

Today is now. Today is a beautifully wrapped present from God waiting for you to open it and enjoy. He delights in you; take joy in him and the time he has given you. From the moment you wake until the time you close your eyes, focus on unwrapping joy.

≫ When you first awaken, thank God for the day that lies ahead. Before drifting off to sleep, recount all the unexpected delights the day held and thank him again.

#17

Enjoy What You Have

How many times have you been struck by if-only-itis? *If only I had a convertible, I would be happy. If only I could get that job, I know I would feel fulfilled. If only he would love me, I would never need anything again.* Concentrating on what you want but don't have robs you of the joy you could be experiencing right now.

Part of God's purpose for your life is your learning to be content with what he has given you. It is okay to want to reach for something more, as long as that something more is more of him.

enjoy

> *Happiness consists more in small conveniences or pleasures that occur every day, than in great pieces of good fortune that happen but seldom to a man in the course of his life.*
>
> Benjamin Franklin

>> Write down a list of all your blessings. Meditate on them and give thanks for them today.

#18

Test Yourself

> LORD, try me and
> test me; look closely
> into my heart
> and mind.
>
> Psalm 26:2 NCV

test

When searching for God's purpose for your life, it is important to slide the cruise control switch to the off position and test your brakes. Are you willing to allow God to grab the steering wheel of your life and guide you in the direction he wants you to go?

Let God press the accelerator—or apply the brakes—throughout your day. Deliberately take yourself off automatic pilot rather than simply coasting through life's tasks. Ask God to do the steering. Test your ability to give up the control, and go with enthusiasm wherever he leads, or stay away from wherever he says not to go.

≫ Take stock of the areas in life where you have been coasting. Determine to take yourself off automatic pilot and allow God into the driver's seat.

#19

Expect the Difficulties

Those who seek God's purpose for their lives will find it, but they will also find trials and challenges along the way. In fact, the Bible promises that troubles will come, but it also guarantees that God will be there to guide you through each one.

The only time to really grow spiritually is during difficulties. When life is smooth, it is too easy to forget your need for God. But when the bottom falls out, people turn to their Creator, looking instinctively to him for comfort, support, and hope. He always provides, and matures his people along the way.

expect

> *The good, the bad, hardship, joy, tragedy, love, and happiness are all interwoven into one indescribable whole that one calls life. You cannot separate the good from the bad, and perhaps there is no need to do so.*
>
> Jacqueline Bouvier Kennedy Onassis

>> Picture the most difficult challenge in your life today. Write down any positive thing you think God could be teaching you through it. Post it where you will see it, as a reminder to ask him to help you through it.

#20

Find Strength in Numbers

> *If we walk in the light, as He is in the light, we have fellowship with one another; and the blood of Jesus Christ His Son cleanses us from all sin.*
>
> 1 John 1:7 MKJV

strength

Faith can become weak when left on its own to grow. God created family and friends for fellowship, and he directs you to find strength among those who share your faith. There is value in gathering with others of similar beliefs whether you attend a weekend conference, go to a Sunday or midweek worship service, or join a Bible study.

God designed you with a longing to be accepted and connected. Fellowship with those on the same course in life—like the friends who joined Christian on *The Pilgrim's Progress* to the Celestial City—makes the road easier. You will find God's purpose for you by getting plugged in.

≫ Join a small study group or sit on a committee at your church. You will find that you strengthen your faith when you surround yourself with others who share your convictions.

#21

Make a Difference

Like the ripple effect when a pebble lands in a lake, so your kindness extends beyond your own initial effort. When you do something that benefits someone else, you forget about your own troubles. That's the nice thing about giving. Making a positive difference for someone today also leaves a legacy of kindness that can be passed on to others.

Making a difference in someone's life can be as small as listening to a lonely person on the phone or as big as volunteering to build a much-needed community project. Examine the positive difference you make in others' lives, and build your legacy beginning today.

difference

> *I expect to pass through life but once. If therefore there be any kindness I can show, or any good thing I can do to any fellow being, let me do it now, and not defer or neglect it, as I shall not pass this way again.*
>
> **William Penn**

≫ Think of a community organization like the Salvation Army or the Humane Society that could use your help today. Volunteer a few hours, or call and ask what supplies they need and donate some.

#22

Visit the Past

> *Remember the days of old; consider the generations long past.*
>
> Deuteronomy 32:7
> NIV

past

It took all of your past—the good and the bad—to mature you into the person you are today. Trials kept you leaning on God. Good times allowed you to rejoice in the beauty of his creation and the life he has given you. Honoring the past, but not dwelling on it, enables you to appreciate the marvelous memories and avoid making the same mistakes again.

Walk down memory lane and recall the beginning of your relationship with God. What challenges have you overcome? What joys did you experience? Thank him for all that he has done and all that he will do with you.

≫ Look at old scrapbooks or photo albums and remember when you first came to know God. Ask him to bring you even closer in your relationship with him today.

#23

Set God-Given Goals

You can accomplish only a limited number of many tasks in the twenty-four hours you are given each day, so wisdom is needed to choose the most important. Determining your priorities helps ensure that you are working toward the purpose God designed you to achieve. Consider where God wants you to be next week, next year, even ten years from now.

Setting goals gives life structure, discipline, and purpose. It helps you focus on the important instead of just on the immediate. Ask God what his goals are for you not only for today but for the rest of your life.

goals

> *Goals determine what you are going to be.*
>
> Julius Erving

≫ Sit down and list your goals for today. Then make a list of goals for one year, five years, and ten years from now. Pray for wisdom in achieving the purpose God designed for you.

#24

Give Graciously

> Let each one give as he purposes in his heart, not grudgingly or of necessity; for God loves a cheerful giver.
>
> 2 Corinthians 9:7
> NKJV

give

It is the right thing to give graciously. It delights the heart of God. You delight the heart of God as you seek God's purpose by happily sacrificing something you have or want for someone else.

God demonstrated many times how to give without counting the cost. He graciously gave the Garden of Eden to Adam and Eve. He gave Jesus to all humankind when he came to Earth to die on the cross. God gave you his best, and he gave it without worrying about what it cost him. He gave with joy. Find your purpose by giving graciously to others.

≫ Give something you value highly to someone else today, without prompting and with a grateful heart. Explain that it is a gift in gratitude for all you have been given.

#25

Consider the Children

Young children at play create a snapshot of the sheer wonder that life holds. Think of the smiles on their faces, the noisy abandon, their sheer enthusiasm, and the sensitivity they openly display.

When children wanted to meet Jesus, his disciples tried to shoo them away. Although he was probably tired and the kids likely caused a commotion, he gathered them close. Then he told his followers that they would be better suited for his service if they became more like the children. The next time you find yourself taking life too seriously, consider the children. Ask God to revive your passion for his purpose.

consider

Catch on fire with enthusiasm and people will come for miles to watch you burn.

John Wesley

≫ Watch children at play today. Catch their enthusiasm for life.

#26

Educate Yourself

> *If you have good sense, instruction will help you to have even better sense. And if you live right, education will help you to know even more.*
>
> Proverbs 9:9 CEV

educate

It's never too late to start learning—or to increase your knowledge. Part of your purpose is to gain the education needed to carry out the tasks for which God designed you. Natural talent is wonderful, but skills that are sharpened through study can often accomplish more.

Today there are opportunities to gain more education, in virtually any area you choose, right at your fingertips. But information remains useless unless it is put to work. If you have not learned anything new lately, head to the library or grab your keyboard and get to work using your skills to find God's purpose for your life.

≫ Research one new aspect of your job, your area of expertise, or your favorite hobby today.

#27

Give God Your Best

It is easy to drift, floating on top of the waves and exerting minimum effort to get to where you are going. Going through life that way can be easy until a storm comes along that threatens to put you under. Then drifting suddenly transforms into something life-threatening.

God created you to reach your fullest potential by exerting effort to swim against the tide. Striving for excellence requires both hands moving through the waters of life and a steady determination to get where you are going. You'll be better prepared for storms if you do. Give it your best shot, and don't settle for anything less.

best

> *I do the very best I know how — the very best I can; and I mean to keep doing so until the end.*
>
> Abraham Lincoln

≫ Before you drift off to sleep tonight, review your day with God. Ask him where you could have exerted more effort to do a better job.

#28

Sing a New Song

> *I will be happy because of you; God Most High, I will sing praises to your name.*
>
> Psalm 9:2 NCV

sing

Sometimes you just need to sing. A song makes your step lighter, keeps your face smiling, and makes your purpose easier to see. Part of God's purpose for you is to sing joyously. David—the writer of many psalms and described by God as a "man after his own heart"—sang many praises to God even in the toughest times.

Life's challenges can rob you of your song just when you need it the most. Don't let them. A song can bring a renewed sense of peace and a deep-down knowledge that God is in control. Sing a joyful song to God today.

>> Look up the lyrics to a favorite song, or learn the words to a new praise song today. Sing it joyously to God.

#29
Lean on Him

In the children's story of the Little Red Hen, the hen decides one day to bake bread from scratch. Her friends won't help her, so she makes it all by herself. She depends on no one else to get the job done.

Too often it is easy to be like the Little Red Hen, shouldering life's burdens and trying to get it all done by yourself. God's purpose for you is to lean your life on him, to relax against him, to stop trying to do it all yourself, and to let him shoulder the load. Then he can guide you to find your unique purpose.

lean

Dependence upon God makes heroes of ordinary people like you and me!

Bruce Wilkinson

≫ Unpack one specific worry onto God's shoulders today. Determine not to concentrate on coming up with your own solution. Let God handle it.

#30
Observe Creation

> Consider the work of
> God: who can make
> straight what He has
> made crooked?
>
> Ecclesiastes 7:13 AMP

observe

Purpose abounds in creation. The monarch butterfly struggles with purpose to loosen its orange-and-black wings from the confines of the cocoon and fly. The ant moves constantly, filled with the purpose of gathering food and building its colony. God intricately fashioned everything in nature to fulfill a purpose. He also has one for you.

Watch a butterfly flit today. See how a bird flies determinedly back and forth to build a nest. Look around you at the wonders of nature, and you can rest assured that God designed you, too, with a unique purpose in mind. After all, you bear the image of the Creator.

≫ Hunt for a bird's nest or follow a butterfly as it flits from flower to flower. Examine it closely, and marvel at its intricacy of design.

#31

Learn from Mistakes

Someone once said that the definition of *crazy* is doing the same thing over and over without changing anything and expecting a different outcome. Thomas Edison tried more than seven hundred times to make the filament in a light bulb work before he had success, but he wasn't crazy. He was learning. He made mistakes and changed direction until he found what worked.

It is perfectly okay to make mistakes. Messing up means you tried, and messing up refines your purpose and potential. The crucial factor is to learn from your errors. Grow from them. Take the lesson learned and apply it the next time.

learn

> *All men make mistakes, but only wise men learn from their mistakes.*
> **Winston Churchill**

≫ Try a new computer program or recipe today. If you mess up, accept that you stepped out of your comfort zone and tried something new. Then try again.

embrace

101 ways to

enjoy

go

seek

gather

find God's purpose
for your life

plug in

recall

achieve

#32

Enter into Worship

> *Worship the LORD with reverence and rejoice with trembling.*
>
> Psalm 2:11 NASB

worship

In the best-selling book *The Purpose Driven Life* by Rick Warren, the author surmises that human beings' main reason for existence is to worship the One who made them.

Everything in your life should be seen as an act of worship, an act that aligns with God's purposes for you, whether that purpose is to drive children to school or to stand in a church pew. Worship requires a change of perception, an altering of the mind-set to determine that everything done be an act of honoring the divine. That kind of attitude can change your life and the lives around you.

>> Make every small task today a conscious act of worship. Pray as you go.

#33

Look Up, Not Down

In order to learn to type well, you must train yourself not to look down at the keys. The same is true for mastering skills like playing the piano. The focus must be in front of you; you can't look down. Looking up allows you to see the whole picture and understand what God has purposed for you.

When life is challenging and difficult, it is easy to look down, but only when you look up can you see the road ahead and find God's purpose for your life. Looking in both directions at once is impossible. When life throws a curve ball, look up.

look

> *I try to avoid looking forward or backward, and try to keep looking upward.*
>
> Charlotte Brontë

≫ Take a sketch pad, go outside, and look up. Draw what you see without looking down. Ask God to reveal his purpose for you as you look up toward him.

#34

Become a Seed Planter

> *The kingdom of heaven is like a mustard seed, which a man took and sowed in his field; and this is smaller than all other seeds, but when it is full grown, it is larger than the garden plants and becomes a tree, so that the birds of the air come and nest in its branches.*
>
> Matthew 13:31–32
> NASB

planter

Johnny "Appleseed" Chapman spent almost fifty years of his life walking around in the American wilderness planting apple seeds. He started apple orchards in Illinois, Indiana, Kentucky, Pennsylvania, and Ohio. After two hundred years, some of those trees still bear fruit, all because of Johnny Appleseed's dream for a land where apple trees were everywhere and no one was hungry. His life made an impact and left a legacy.

You are designed to be a planter of seeds—seeds of hope, seeds of love, seeds of joy, and seeds of faith. Seize the opportunities to share the great things God has done for you.

≫ Bite into a crunchy apple today and remember the work of Johnny Appleseed, and then look for ways to plant seeds of joy, hope, or love in someone's life.

#35

Take Good Advice

Imagine the quarterback for an NFL team standing on the football field alone. When it was time to snap the ball, where would he throw it? No matter how good that quarterback is, he needs the team in order to fulfill his purpose and play the game. He needs the coach to guide him.

Words of wisdom from one close friend to another are words to refine. Friends stand with you as God coaches you toward finding and fulfilling your purpose. In order for a team to win, the players must listen to one another, heed other players' good advice, and follow the directions of the coach.

advice

Build for your team a feeling of oneness, of dependence on one another and of strength to be derived by unity.

Vince Lombardi

≫ Ask close friends to be your accountability partners to share and pray together regularly and to keep you on the path of fulfilling God's purpose for your lives.

#36

Get Away with God

> *Afterward he went up into the hills by himself to pray. Night fell while he was there alone.*
>
> Matthew 14:23 NLT

away

When Jesus was spiritually drained, he left the company of his disciples or his followers and went off alone to spend time with God. He prayed; he wept; he was tempted. He recharged his batteries in the wilderness by himself more than once.

It is time to learn from the Master. Take time away from ordinary activities to spend time solely focused on God, to allow him to speak to you and reveal his purpose for you. Spend time communing together, whether it is in a corner of a bedroom or out walking in the woods. He longs to be with you; make room for him.

≫ Plan a spiritual retreat for a day or a weekend in the next two months to a bed-and-breakfast, a nearby hotel, or a Christian camp. Put it on the calendar today.

#37

Read Great Works

Reading about someone's faith and redemption can help you find your purpose and strengthen your own experience with God. Great literary works of the faith give fresh perspective and another way of looking at what you believe. Part of God's purpose for you is to prompt you to learn from others.

Through the centuries, great thinkers have left behind a legacy that can enlighten readers to great truths. Leaders of the faith often faced persecution, trials, and tribulations. Pick up a great work and peel back the truth on the pages one layer at a time; drink it in, and apply it to your life.

read

> *A book is a garden, an orchard, a storehouse, a party, a company by the way, a counselor, a multitude of counselors.*
>
> Henry Ward Beecher

≫ Pick up a copy of C. S. Lewis's *Mere Christianity* or John Bunyan's *The Pilgrim's Progress* and read it.

#38

Let Go of Grudges

> *Don't let the sun go down on your anger.*
>
> Ephesians 4:26 HCSB

let go

Making peace with the past can give you a renewed sense of purpose, a lighter step, and a healed heart. Everyone knows people who cannot let go of the hurts they experienced. Their bitterness shows on their faces; it comes out in their talk; it reveals itself in their actions. Nurturing unresolved anger toward someone who hurt you creates infection in the victim, not the perpetrator.

In order to see clearly God's purpose for your life, you have to take off the glasses of old hurts. Ask God to reveal any resentment you might be harboring, and then get rid of it once and for all.

>> Think of someone who hurt you, and ask God to remove the pain. Forgive that person, and ask God to heal your hurt once and for all. He will.

#39

Set the Example

Set a good example for those following behind, whether your friends, family, colleagues, or simply strangers you meet in public. Finding God's purpose for you involves being the light in dark places, determining to be the flavor of life to a dying world. You also find his purpose when your life shows tangible evidence to those around you that God exists and works to change lives today.

Determine to make your life an example of his love. Practice kindness, courtesy, thoughtfulness, honesty, and generosity. People around you will see him in you, and you will be a means to strengthen their faith.

example

> A baptism of holiness, a demonstration of godly living is the crying need of our day.
>
> Duncan Campbell

>> Read the New Testament book of Ephesians, chapters 4–6. Write down the ways God wants you to fulfill your purpose by living as an example of his love.

#40

Remember His Story

She gave birth to her Son, her Firstborn; and she wrapped Him in swaddling clothes and laid Him in a manger, because there was no room or place for them in the inn.

Luke 2:7 AMP

remember

You can find God's purpose for your life as you learn his story and recognize that you, too, are part of it. Think about the creation of the earth, the coming of God's Son, Jesus, through the virgin birth, and his death and resurrection. It is all for you.

God's purpose for you revolves around learning this history—his story—and the hope you can have for life eternal. You are so important to him that he wrote it down just for you. Get to know his story, and ask him what he would write in the chapter of your life.

≫ Over the next thirty days, read through the four Gospels of Matthew, Mark, Luke, and John, asking God to illuminate through Christ's story his purpose for you.

#41

Celebrate His Life

God's purpose for your life can be found not only in learning about God's story, but also in celebrating the richness of Christ's life and patterning yours after it. When Jesus wanted to have an impact on lives, he showed love. Where some would uphold the law, Christ extended grace. He extends it to you, so that you can share it with others.

God's purpose for you is to follow the example of Jesus with excitement and enthusiasm, to glory in the celebration of his life and your own. Put on a party hat, place a candle on a cupcake, and celebrate life with Jesus today.

celebrate

I can't imagine more surprising places for God to appear than a manger or a cross. Yet all through his life and resurrection, Jesus demonstrates the power of showing and sharing God's love.

Fred Rogers

>> Celebrate God's purpose for your life by doing some of your favorite things today.

#42

Determine Your Gifts

> *We all have different gifts, each of which came because of the grace God gave us.*
>
> Romans 12:6 NCV

gifts

God gave you some very special gifts. He gave you unique abilities that you can use to help others and to find and fulfill the purpose for which God designed you. Your gifts may be in administration, philanthropy, evangelism, hospitality, music, or many other areas.

Your gifts are like presents under a Christmas tree. They are beautiful to look at, but their usefulness lies inside. It is impossible to use a gift until it has been opened. By determining what your spiritual gifts are, you open the present God has given you, and you can fulfill his purpose for you by putting your gifts to work.

>> Go online and find a spiritual gifts test or ask your church for one. Use it to help determine your special gifts.

#43

Listen Carefully

Listening takes skill. It is easy to run right in with advice; it is far more difficult to put the advice on a shelf and just let someone talk. Too often in life people are unable to logically formulate a plan to overcome their difficulties. Too many people told them how to do it before they had a chance to figure it out themselves. Too many people feel alone, even in the midst of a crowd, because everyone wants to talk to them but no one takes the time to hear them.

Practice listening to others and to God. It will make a positive difference in your life as well as in theirs.

listen

> It is the province of knowledge to speak, and it's a privilege of wisdom to listen.
>
> Oliver Wendell Holmes

≫ When someone shares a story today, just listen. Be attentive and caring, and let him or her talk through it.

#44

Laugh Out Loud

> A cheerful heart is good medicine, but a crushed spirit dries up the bones.
>
> Proverbs 17:22 NIV

laugh

Laughter helps strengthen your body and keeps it healthy. Laughing lowers blood pressure, reduces stress hormones, increases muscle flexibility, and boosts immune functions by raising levels of infection-fighting cells and proteins. Laughter even triggers the release of endorphins, the body's natural painkillers, and produces a general sense of well-being.

Studies show that children laugh eighty to a hundred times a day, while adults may laugh ten times or less in a twenty-four-hour period. You face life with a better outlook and sense of purpose when you have a merry heart.

≫ Look in the mirror and repeat the verse above. After that, find a funny joke to tell today, and laugh whenever you can.

#45

Learn About Heaven

Heaven is touted as a wonderful place, the place where God lives and reigns. It is paved with streets of gold, but do you know much more about it than that? If you will spend eternity in heaven, part of your purpose is to educate yourself about where you are headed.

The book of Revelation says that heaven will be a joyous place. It states that there will be no more death, crying, or pain. Thinking about a pain-free life in a beautiful place with God brings joy, peace of mind, and excitement, and those are all characteristics of a life that is living God's purpose.

heaven

When all the world dissolves, and every creature shall be purified, all places shall be hell that are not heaven.

Christopher Marlowe

>> Read different theologians' perspectives and descriptions of heaven, and dive into the Bible book of Revelation, chapters 19 and 21, to find some answers for yourself.

#46

Seek Ye First

> *Seek first the kingdom of God and his righteousness, and all these things will be added to you.*
>
> Matthew 6:33 ESV

seek

Jesus instructed those listening to him to find their purpose by looking first for the kingdom of God. He promised that if they did, they would receive it—and lots more. He pointed out that people should not worry about their own needs. Those things will be taken care of if you have your priorities straight.

The act of seeking points to a person's motivation for living. You seek something when you want to have it. You desire it, you need it, and you are looking for it. That is the heart attitude Jesus desires, a longing to find him and his kingdom.

>> Tell Jesus that you want his help in seeking his kingdom first. Ask him to help you adjust your focus toward him.

#47

Take a Break

Take a well-deserved break to reevaluate the ways you are working to find God's purpose for your life. When you put away the calendars, cell phones, and electronic organizers and take a temporary time-out from bosses, kids, and in-boxes, you can experience a fresh sense of determination and realign priorities.

Even if you can't physically get away, build in breaks from the noise. Put away the gadgets that go with modern-day life and renew your goal to find God's purpose for you. Take long walks, study Scripture, schedule prayer times, and plan fellowship with friends.

r e l a x

> *Every now and then go away, have a little relaxation, for when you come back to your work your judgment will be surer.*
>
> Leonardo da Vinci

>>Take a mini-break today by leaving the cell phone, iPod, and PDA behind and adding a quiet walk to your lunch break. Then add an extended vacation time to your calendar.

worship

101 ways to

focus

plant

follow

commune

find God's purpose for your life

apply

find

recognize

#48

Entertain Angels

Do not forget to entertain strangers, for by so doing some have unwittingly entertained angels.

Hebrews 13:2 NKJV

angels

In the television series *Touched by an Angel*, angels lived on earth to protect people and prompt them to do good deeds. The series was not far-fetched. The Bible says that you never know when you might be entertaining an angel. There are countless stories of people who appeared out of nowhere to meet a desperate need and then disappeared just as quickly.

Look for needs around you that you can meet. Find joy lending a hand in unexpected places. You are finding God's purpose when you go out of your way for others, and you might entertain an angel while you're at it.

≫ Go out of your way to look for a need to meet today. Offer assistance to a single mom, repair a broken computer or a car, or listen to a hurting soul.

#49

Find a Church That Fits

People of faith need other people of faith. God designed you that way. The church can be the jumping-off point to a deeper relationship with God and with others who share your beliefs and seek God's purpose.

When you connect to a church, you receive opportunities to grow, and you give of yourself. The local church you choose may need an administrator like you, an evangelist like you, a musician like you, or even a seamstress or carpenter like you. The church finds its purpose by meeting needs on earth and bringing others to Jesus through you, and you find your purpose by sharing your gifts.

church

The Church is the hidden Christ among us.

Dietrich Bonhoeffer

≫ Go to church this Sunday. If you are a regular, look for new ways to get involved. If you haven't been in a while, ask God to guide you to just the right place.

#50

Celebrate Jesus' Birth

> The angel said,
> "Don't be afraid! I
> have good news for
> you, which will make
> everyone happy. This
> very day in King
> David's hometown
> a Savior was born
> for you. He is Christ
> the Lord."
>
> Luke 2:10–11 CEV

celebrate

When Jesus came to earth as a baby, the heavens celebrated. Angels appeared and sang joyously to announce the good news to shepherds tending their flocks in the countryside. Part of finding God's purpose for you is to reconnect with the thrill of Jesus' coming and joyously celebrate his birth all year.

The miracle of Jesus lies not only in the virgin birth, the appearance of the star, and the Magi traveling to worship him. The real miracle is wrapped up in the heart of a God who would leave a perfect, heavenly throne to become a man, feel your pain, and share your experiences.

>> Find God's purpose for you by reconnecting with the story of Jesus' birth. Read Luke 2. Then celebrate his birth today.

#51

Stand Up Straight

Standing up straight is a simple act that conveys a lot. For instance, it displays self-confidence. When you walk with head up, shoulders back, and a smile on your face, you command attention and respect. Prepare yourself to find God's purpose for you by standing up straight, making eye contact with those around you, and sharing the source of your joy and enthusiasm for life.

Standing tall and walking with a spring in your step will make others want to know, "What does that person have that I don't?" When they ask, tell them God has a purpose for you and for them, too.

stand

> *When you do the common things in life in an uncommon way, you will command the attention of the world.*
>
> George Washington Carver

>> Walk with enthusiasm today, smiling and making eye contact with those you pass. Find God's purpose for you by sharing with others the faith and assurance that you possess.

#52

Hand Over the Control

> *You guide me with your counsel, and afterward you will receive me to glory.*
>
> Psalm 73:24 ESV

control

God gives you the free will to make your own choices, but he is hoping you will let him guide and direct you, gently steering you away from the rocks. In order for you to sail the course he has charted, however, you have to let him be the captain.

Handing over control is a big part of God's purpose for your life. He wants to do great things through you, but he waits for you to give yourself to him willingly. Before you try to wrestle with life's challenges to find your own solutions, ask God how he wants you to solve them.

≫ Ask God to show you the direction you should take to figure out the solution to your biggest problem.

#53

Smile a Lot

The only way to have true joy is to remember to put *J*esus first, *o*thers second, *y*ourself last. When you remember to arrange your actions in that order, you can truly experience *J-o-y* and find and fulfill God's purpose for your life by expressing it with a big smile.

Some people have *y-o-J*, putting themselves first and Jesus last. Others have just *y-o*, without Jesus in the equation at all. And there are more than a few people who have plain old *y*. Your purpose in life is to smile a lot, singing God's praises. Aim for *Joy*, and you will get it.

smile

> *You're a happy fellow, for you'll give happiness and joy to many other people. There is nothing better or greater than that!*
>
> Ludwig van Beethoven

≫ Share the joy God gives you with others. Put on a smile, and make sure you wear it throughout the day.

#54

Ask the Hard Questions

The spiritual man tries all things [he examines, investigates, inquires into, questions, and discerns all things].

1 Corinthians 2:15
AMP

ask

Life is not easy, and the Christian life is no exception. God knows that you will have questions, doubts, and fears during the hard times. Part of finding God's purpose for you is to recognize that he can handle your hard questions, and that he wants you to ask them to draw you into closer relationship with him.

When difficulties come, you can pull away from God or you can choose to draw as close as you can, seeking answers to life's hard questions by searching Scripture, praying fervently, and standing on God's promises. When you ask, you offer him the opportunity to answer.

≫ Take your toughest questions to the Lord today. Ask him to reveal his purpose for you through these puzzles and challenges so your relationship with him can grow stronger.

#55

Watch God Work

God works to fulfill his purpose in your life and the lives of those around you all the time. God's imprint is visible everywhere—from the indescribable hues of an early morning sunrise to the unexplainable peace after prayer in the midst of crisis.

When you pray for a situation's outcome, you should remember to watch for God's hand at work in your life. Praying requires faith, and faith demands expectancy. Those who believe that God has a purpose for their lives must lie in wait to catch him in the act and remember to thank him mightily for the great deeds he has done.

watch

If you begin to live life looking for the God that is all around you, every moment becomes a prayer.

Frank Bianco

≫ Get a notebook and journal the ways you are seeking God's purpose and how and what he reveals to you along the way. Date each effort, and review your growth regularly.

#56

Teach Your Family

> Go home to your family and tell them how much the Lord has done for you, and how he has had mercy on you.
>
> Mark 5:19 NIV

teach

Faith passed down creates a legacy of spiritual strength that can have an impact on the world. Whether you are a parent, somebody's child or grandchild, or a member of a family of friends, you can make an eternal difference in their lives by sharing the truth of God's love that you have found in your own life.

In order to find God's purpose for your life, share him with the family he has entrusted to you. Open up with your parent, sister, son, cousin, grandfather, or daughter and explain how God makes a difference in your life. You can forever change theirs.

≫ Find God's purpose for your life by sharing with a family member the difference your faith makes in your life.

#57

Be Willing to Move

Digging up a tree that you planted, especially a tree that has rooted well, takes a lot of work. Usually a tree can bloom, bear fruit, and die in one spot only. God desires for you to grow and bear fruit, but he may want you to spread your faith far and wide and not remain rooted in one place.

Does God desire for you to move? Are you doing the right job, living in the right community, sharing your faith in the right places? You may accomplish more of God's purpose if you pursue his direction, whether it is to be uprooted or to stay where you are.

move

> *Even if you're on the right track you'll get run over if you just sit there.*
>
> Will Rogers

≫ Examine where you live, work, and fellowship. Pledge to be willing to take a chance and move wherever God wants to plant you to do his work.

#58

Love the Unlovable

> *I will call those who were not My people, "My people," and her who was not beloved, "Beloved."*
>
> Romans 9:25 NASB

love

You find God's purpose for your life when you put the needs of others first. The Bible says so again and again in the New Testament. Jesus himself stated that God's command to those who would follow him is to love others above themselves. While it is easy to put the needs of a spouse, a parent, or a child before your own, loving others outside the family circle requires more work.

You find your purpose and honor God when you step out of your comfort zone and act with love, regardless of your feelings. Love in action comforts, demonstrates kindness, and improves the lives of those around you.

≫ Find someone you don't know or don't get along with who could use a boost today. Create a care basket of candies, tea, or other small gifts and drop it off to them, or give them a gift certificate for a meal.

#59

Go on a Retreat

Taking a purposeful retreat from daily life for a period of solitude and reflection can bring a renewed sense of peace and purpose. When the mind and body are active and engaged, the soul often has to wait its turn. God's desire is that you nourish yourself physically, emotionally, intellectually, and spiritually.

A retreat gives your body and mind a chance to be still and quiet, to rest while your spirit awakens to the still, quiet voice of God. Your body and soul will respond to the use of solitude to seek God's presence. Retreat from your normal activities and listen for him.

retreat

> *If you completely give of yourself physically, you become exhausted. But when you give of yourself spiritually, you get more strength.*
>
> Oswald Chambers

≫ Find out from friends or your church about retreats in your area. Schedule a time to retreat from your daily life and reflect on the purpose that God has for you.

#60

Write Out Reminders

> *Commit yourselves completely to these words of mine. Tie them to your hands as a reminder, and wear them on your forehead. . . . Write them on the doorposts of your house and on your gates.*
>
> Deuteronomy 11:18–20 NLT

write

God's purpose for you may seem clear when you are in the midst of Bible study or prayer. However, the feeling that you are doing the right things, accomplishing what he wants for you, and loving and being loved can escape under the pressures of daily life.

Written reminders of God's love, his faithfulness, and your purpose can keep you on track throughout your days. Write out special Bible verses, favorite quotes, answers to prayer, and revelations that God has given you. Post them around your desk or carry them with you, and they will keep you headed in the right direction.

>> Write out a verse that encourages you, insert your name in it as if God is saying it directly to you, and post it where you will see it daily and be reminded of God's purpose for you.

#61

Read Through the Word

God reveals himself in myriad ways throughout the Bible. The Bible is God's inspired book and the guide for life for those who believe in him. You can get to know the character of God and his expectations for your life by reading the Bible faithfully and completely.

Each book in the Bible was divinely inspired and included as a blueprint for you to follow. Many books are familiar, but some may be new to you. There are several good plans for reading the Bible. You might want to read all the way through the Bible, from the first book, Genesis, to the last book, Revelation.

read

> *We may be certain that whatever God has made prominent in his word, he intended to be conspicuous in our lives.*
>
> Charles Spurgeon

≫ Implement a reading plan that will take you all the way through the Bible, and ask God to reveal his purpose for you.

#62

Don't Jump the Gun

> *Wait on the LORD;*
> *be of good courage,*
> *and He shall*
> *strengthen your*
> *heart; wait, I say,*
> *on the LORD!*
>
> Psalm 27:14 NKJV

jump

Sometimes God answers prayer right away. Often, however, God may delay his answer until the right time for everything to fall into place. Until you know God's answer, you may wonder what direction to take. At such times, your role may be simply to sit back and wait.

This life is just a blink in the eye of eternity, and you can be assured that God sees down the road. If you wait, the One who loves you perfectly can guide the situation to its optimal outcome. In times when you have to wait, God will be with you all the way.

≫ Put any urgent matter on hold until God has given you clear direction. No matter what your deadline is, God has a purpose for the delay.

#63

Ask for Forgiveness

If you bump into somebody, step on his toes, or spill milk down his shirt, saying "I'm sorry" indicates your regret. In an accident, a simple "I'm sorry" makes amends. In cases where your action or attitude purposely hurtful, it heals hearts to say not only "I'm sorry" but also "Will you forgive me?" You honor the one you have hurt by humbling yourself and having a repentant heart.

If you have purposely wronged someone, examine your motives and your heart, repent, and seek forgiveness from the other person and from God. God can use your repentant heart to heal another's hardened heart.

ask

> *Forgiveness is the giving, and so the receiving, of life.*
>
> George MacDonald

≫ Ask those you have wronged to forgive you. Take time to ask God to forgive you for the wrongs you have done as well.

entertain

101 ways to

share

reconnect

stand up

hand over

find God's purpose for your life

smile

draw close

remember

#64

Take Communion

> [Jesus] blessed the bread and broke it. Then he gave it to his disciples and said, "Take this and eat it. This is my body." Jesus picked up a cup of wine and gave thanks to God. He then gave it to his disciples and said, "Take this and drink it. This is my blood, and with it God makes his agreement with you. It will be poured out, so that many people will have their sins forgiven."
>
> Matthew 26:26–28
> CEV

When you partake in Holy Communion, you show honor to Jesus for his sacrifice of dying on the cross. At the Last Supper, Jesus began the Communion himself and instructed his disciples and followers to continue it. He broke bread and gave the disciples pieces of it, then passed a cup of wine for them to drink. He told them to remember him in the future when they ate and drank.

The disciples did not grasp the price Jesus was about to pay, so he gave remembrances for them to recapture the magnitude of his suffering and sacrifice. Take Communion to remember what he did for you.

≫ Find a church that offers the sacrament of Communion, and do this in remembrance of him, prayerfully seeking his purpose for your life.

#65

Work Diligently

The work you do paints a picture of the kind of person you are. Work hard and put your best efforts forward. You are receptive to finding God's purpose for your life when you use your gifts and talents, strive daily, reach for your potential, and show others the rewards of giving your best to each task throughout each day.

In everything you do, dedicate yourself to working hard at it—the parts that come naturally and the parts that stretch you beyond your comfort zone. When you work diligently, people notice when they see him in you. Hard workers are valued and appreciated.

work

> *Laziness may appear attractive, but work gives satisfaction.*
>
> Anne Frank

≫ Go back over recent work that you have done and make sure you covered all the bases. Then go about today's projects with renewed vigor and diligence to demonstrate God's presence in your life and his purpose for you.

#66

Hand Out Compliments

> *She opens her mouth with wisdom, and on her tongue is the law of kindness.*
>
> Proverbs 31:26 NKJV

compliment

Sincere compliments change the atmosphere in a workplace or home. Making someone's day can be as easy as stopping to comment on her new haircut, the shirt she is wearing, or the good job she is doing. Compliments benefit the giver and the receiver, and are a clear extension of God's love.

When you compliment others, you obey God's command that you act with kindness and yield yourself to God's guidance. Compliments are an extension of God's call on you to love. They are good medicine for the soul and keep you pointed in the right direction, so hand out compliments freely.

≫ Tell your children, your spouse, your friends, or your coworkers how proud you are of them today. Compliment something they are doing well.

#67

Stand Still Sometimes

Sometimes God's purpose for you stems from standing still and allowing his glorious presence to wash over you. If you are always in a hurry, you can miss the blessings God has purposed for you to experience and enjoy.

Standing still means noticing the smell of fresh bread from the bakery, taking in the vibrant colors of a rose beginning to bloom, and savoring the taste of that fresh coffee or bagel with cream cheese. When you stand still, you can give God all your attention and fully seek his purpose without distraction, allowing him to show you the good things he has for you.

still

Learn to labor and to wait.

Henry Wadsworth Longfellow

>> Stop on a street corner today and observe the hustle and bustle around you. Ask God to show you his purpose for you as you stand still and think of him in the middle of a busy day.

#68

Learn "Love Languages"

> *If I could speak in any language in heaven or on earth but didn't love others, I would only be making meaningless noise like a loud gong or a clanging cymbal.*
>
> 1 Corinthians 13:1
> NLT

learn

In order to learn "love languages," learn the ways that people feel loved. Some people get the head rush of love when others perform acts of service for them, like taking out the garbage. Some people feel loved when others shower gifts on them, while still other people enjoy words of encouragement, physical touch, or quality time spent together.

Loving others in your own love language is a cinch. Simply think of things that would make you feel loved and do them. Love for others will often lead you to find God's purpose for you. Discover the love languages of others and make sure you speak their language.

>> Speak your love language for others by performing an act of service, giving a gift, spending time, giving a loving touch, or praising them.

#69

Turn Off the Noise

Today, people regularly do several activities at once—talk on the phone, instant-message, pay bills, surf the Internet—all with the television or radio in the background. With all the electronic noises and distractions, it is no wonder studies show that attention spans are getting shorter and shorter. Focus is harder to find.

Constant noise can drown out contemplation and eliminate the ability to quietly reflect on finding God's purpose for your life. Turn off the noise in your house and listen to the sounds of silence. You may hear the still, small voice of God, trying to share what he has waiting for you.

noise

> *True silence is the rest of the mind; it is to the spirit what sleep is to the body, nourishment and refreshment.*
>
> Sir William Penn

≫ Spend your next free day at home with as little noise as possible. Keep the television and radio off, ignore the computer, and keep conversation to a minimum. Listen for God's voice sharing his purpose for you instead.

#70

Let Anger Out

> Don't sin by letting anger gain control over you.
>
> Psalm 4:4 NLT

anger

What you do with anger—whether you manage it or whether you give in to it—determines how effective you can be in finding your life's purpose. Becoming angry when life is not fair or when people hurt you is natural, but you need to handle it properly.

Acknowledge your anger without letting it control you. In that manner, anger can become an agent for change. The key is to confront your anger and move on. Direct your anger at the injustice and make a positive difference. You will gain insight into your purpose as you control your impulses, learn the lessons that God intends, and practice God's grace.

≫ Ask God to help you make peace with your anger, learn from it, and move forward.

#71

Sacrifice Something

There is great purpose in letting go of something you desire. It requires discipline, and it puts the things you still have in perspective. Sometimes sacrifice prepares you for bigger tasks that lie ahead. Sometimes it gives you empathy to relate to others who are giving up the same things.

Letting go of what you love clears the way to discover what God has in mind for you. By so doing you show God that nothing is more important to you than he is. Elevate God above the desire to keep things for yourself. Demonstrate your love for God and his position as number one by being willing to sacrifice.

sacrifice

> *He who would accomplish little need sacrifice little; he who would achieve much must sacrifice much. He who would attain highly must sacrifice greatly.*
>
> James Allen

≫ Choose something that you love but are willing to give up for a week, a month, or the rest of your life and let this be a reminder of God's sacrifice for you.

#72

Play for a Day

I recommend having fun, because there is nothing better for people to do in this world than to eat, drink, and enjoy life. That way they will experience some happiness along with all the hard work God gives them.

Ecclesiastes 8:15 NLT

play

A rich life, a fulfilled life, requires play. Recreation time gives the players a chance to be themselves, to uncover the joy of embracing life. Play refreshes, energizes, and clears the mind of worries and the body of tension. God thrills to see your joy, so you can take time to play as you seek to find his purpose for your life.

Playtime can help you tackle problems with renewed vigor and a fresh outlook. Sometimes you accomplish great things when it seems you are doing little. Take your mind off your challenges for a while and play; new solutions may then become apparent.

≫ Schedule one full day of just playing to allow God to delight in you. Let go of chores, phone calls, e-mails, and work and have some fun!

#73

Keep the Main Focus

Pay attention to and keep sight of what is important as you attend to the details of your daily life. Order your tasks and clear your mind to be alert to learning your God-willed direction and to aim to reach it.

Jesus summed up the main priorities in life when he said that the most important commandments are to love God with all your heart, soul, and strength, and to love your neighbor as yourself. When you keep those words fresh in your mind and act on them, you keep the main focus as you seek to find God's purpose.

focus

The Christian heart, since it has been thoroughly persuaded that all things happen by God's plan, and that nothing takes place by chance, will ever look to him as the principal causes of things, yet will give attention to the secondary causes in their proper place.

John Calvin

≫ Craft a mission statement for your life that sums up what you believe is your main focus. Put it where you can review it regularly.

#74

Get Rid of Guilt

As far as the east is from the west, so far does he remove our transgressions from us.

Psalm 103:12 ESV

guilt

The life that God wants you to live is not a fat-free one but a guilt-free one. God's grace frees you from all guilt, if you lay it down, so that you can be about the business of doing the work God has for you and finding your life's purpose.

The Bible says that God takes your confessed sin and throws it as far as east is from west; he never remembers it again. The past is gone; he wants you to seek to find his purpose for you today. Let go of guilt, and get on with the life of joy he has for you.

≫ Close your eyes and give God anything you have carried guilt about. Visualize standing on a dock and heaving that sack out to sea.

#75

Reach Out to the Lost

You have a unique life story. No one has ever experienced exactly the life that you have. Consider that God's purpose for you may be for you to share your special story and the good things God has done for you. Be willing to tell others about what he has done.

Every day you encounter many hurting people who have no idea who God is or where to find him and talk to him. You may be the only tangible evidence they encounter of God. You can tell them how much he loves them and wants to have a relationship with them. Tell your story to someone today.

lost

Lord, make me an instrument of your peace.
St. Francis of Assisi

≫ Write a letter or e-mail to someone and share your story. Let him or her know that God loves them.

#76

Hold Your Head High

They have bowed down and fallen; but we have risen and stand upright.

Psalm 20:8 NKJV

high

Faith in God requires boldness of purpose, direct eye contact, and a willingness to hold your head high. The way God loves you is awesome, and holding your head high shows him that you know it. Just as you may be proud of your local baseball team or your family's accomplishments and standing in your local community, feel even more the warmth and belonging for God.

Look for God's purpose for you as you go about showing him that you are happy to be someone that he loves. Hold your head high and honor him as you go through life this week.

>> Hold your head high today as you thank God for instilling your life with his purpose and for being among those he loves.

#77

Know Your Neighbors

In days gone by, neighbors used to sit on front porches, talk about their days, watch one another's children, and borrow cups of sugar. There was community, a common bond that gets lost in busy society today.

Look for God's purpose among the people around you. Say "hello" when you meet your neighbors, and engage them in short conversation. Consider that God placed you in a particular place to be neighbors to those particular people. Only you can accomplish what he has for you in those relationships. Extend a hand of friendship to your neighbors and see what God has in store for you.

know

> *Friendship is the only cement that will ever hold the world together.*
>
> Woodrow Wilson

≫ Buy some inexpensive coffee mugs, fill them with cookies, coffee packets, or tea bags and deliver them to your neighbors with an invitation to join you for tea.

#78

Prepare for Greatness

> *Get your minds ready for action, being self-disciplined, and set your hope completely on the grace to be brought to you at the revelation of Jesus Christ.*
>
> 1 Peter 1:13 HCSB

prepare

Military troops go into battle only after getting prepared. New recruits enter grueling basic training where they exercise their bodies, learn to handle weapons, and practice working together as a group. They prepare to do a great job on the battlefield, and some receive medals of highest honor for jobs well done.

God is preparing you for greatness too. He designed you to accomplish things no one else can do. He wants you to live with him for eternity. Step up to the plate and get ready to bat. Prepare for God's greatness, and be confident that he can and will use you to your potential.

>> Choose a long-term goal to prepare yourself for God's purpose. Prepare yourself to do the work needed to achieve the goal.

#79

Grow Through Grief

God does not always reveal the purpose for disappointments and pain that you experience in your life, but he does show the way to the other side of grief if you lean on him. Pain strips your defenses and brings you to your knees, where the only place to find hope and comfort is in his arms.

Allow grief to strengthen you and foster growth. Like the refiner's fire, grief burns away the dross and leaves you scorched but gleaming and ready to be used for his glory. Know that whatever happens, God is with you and can use your experiences for his glory.

grow

> We must accept finite disappointment, but we must never lose infinite hope.
>
> Martin Luther King Jr.

≫ Reflect on the losses you have had in life. Make a list of the lessons learned from your disappointments and tragedies. Keep it as a milestone marker of your passage through grief.

grow

101 ways to

work

compliment

notice

love

find God's purpose
for your life

contemplate

acknowledge

let go

#80

Extend Grace and Mercy

> *Let us therefore come boldly to the throne of grace, that we may obtain mercy and find grace to help in time of need.*
>
> Hebrews 4:16 NKJV

grace

Every time you extend mercy and grace to the people you encounter in your life, you come that much closer to finding God's purpose. By extending mercy, you show love and genuine care and concern instead of negativity or condemnation. By extending grace, you give something good to someone who does not expect it.

People need to give and receive heaping measures of both mercy and grace, and you glow with God's love when you give them. Extend both mercy and grace to your family, your friends, your neighbors, and to those who least expect it, and you can be an instrument of change in their lives.

≫ Ask God to help you extend mercy and grace in specific situations this week.

#81

Volunteer Your Skills

Applying skills to hard work usually results in the reward of a paycheck or other monetary gain. The money is justified for the effort. The Bible says that a worker is "worthy of his hire." However, there are other rewards that come with offering your skills without expecting payment.

Giving yourself to God so he can reveal his will for you means saying, as the prophet Isaiah did, "Here am I, Lord. Send me." Offering up your talent begins with stating that you are available and that you are a tool waiting to be used by the hand of God.

volunteer

> *When I stand before God at the end of my life, I would hope that I would not have a single bit of talent left and could say, "I used everything you gave me."*
>
> Erma Bombeck

≫ Donate part of your time and your skill this week to a local school, your church, or a single parent you know.

#82

Memorize Scriptures

> *I treasure your word in my heart, so that I may not sin against you.*
>
> Psalm 119:11 NRSV

memorize

Memorizing Scripture gives you a better understanding of the Bible and of the way God wants you to live. The Bible says that you are to hide his word in your heart, and you do this by reading, studying, and inwardly digesting what God has to say.

Intimately knowing Scripture helps you find God's purpose in your life because it is ready and on the tip of your tongue when you face temptation or trials. The verses you know come back to you and remind you to call on God. They help you give him the control, and they comfort you.

≫ Choose one verse or short passage per week to memorize. Copy it, practice saying it aloud, and keep at it until you know it for good.

#83

Take Deep Breaths

To improve your health, experts say that you should take deep breaths every day. Breathing deeply helps dispose of carbon dioxide and prevents toxins from building up. Deep breaths also keep the lungs pure and increase the flow of clean blood, which benefits nerves, brain, spinal cord, and heart muscles.

Stopping to take deep breaths refreshes you. It helps you regroup, think more clearly, and redirect your efforts. Take a deep breath before you act when you face a trial, and let God work through you.

breathe

When your world seems like too much to handle, just take a deep breath and laugh. It clears the mind and frees your spirit.

Author Unknown

≫ Place your hands around your waist, with your fingers touching along your spine and thumbs on your sides. Take slow, deep breaths. Your hands will move apart when you inhale, and back together when you exhale. Repeat several times a day.

#84

Smell a Flower

> *After the wind blows, the flower is gone, and there is no sign of where it was.*
>
> Psalm 103:16 NCV

smell

Stopping to smell a flower can have big benefits. In order to smell a flower, you have to notice that it is there, pause to inhale its fragrance, and marvel at its beauty and intricacy of design.

Since God cared enough to create thousands of types of flowers with individual shapes, colors, and fragrances that live for such a short time, consider how much more he must have a special design and purpose for you. You move toward finding his purpose for you when you stop to appreciate his creation, remind yourself how beautiful you are in his eyes, and are attentive to his marvelous work.

≫ Buy a bouquet of flowers today, and inhale the fragrance deeply. Share it with someone else and invite them to share in the beautiful scent.

#85

Encourage Others

You are designed to encourage other people, and your daily goings-about give you opportunity to practice building up others. Many people need to know they are doing a good job, and they need the reassurance that they can make it through the hard times. When you act as an encourager, you are fulfilling God's command and call on your life.

When you encourage others, it makes a positive difference in their lives and yours, just as God encourages you for doing what he called you to do. Ask God to reveal to you the positives in the people around you so that you can give them confidence.

encourage

> *Those who are lifting the world upward and onward are those who encourage more than criticize.*
>
> Elizabeth Harrison

>> Practice saying words of encouragement to those around you today. Notice the efforts of others and help them aim to do even better.

#86

Look Behind You

> *Whatever exists today and whatever will exist in the future has already existed in the past. For God calls each event back in its turn.*
>
> Ecclesiastes 3:15 NLT

look

Rearview mirrors give you "eyes in the back of your head," a vision of what is happening behind you that you normally could not see. The picture is necessary to stay safe, to make proper judgment calls, and to negotiate traffic. Taking a glance at what is going on behind you enables you to see conditions that might affect your driving ahead.

When you look behind you in life, you are able to evaluate your options more clearly. Looking at the accidents and close calls of your past helps keep you from repeating the same errors. Rearview vision helps you to keep moving forward.

>> Glance in the rearview mirror of your life and examine the major intersections and U-turns. Recall the dead-end streets, and consider what got you turned around again.

#87

Wait Patiently

In an age when information can be found in an instant and food can be heated in seconds, waiting for anything can cause great frustration. Waiting patiently is necessary, however, to receive all that God has for you. Part of finding God's purpose for you is in having the patience to wait for him to reveal it.

He chooses how to show you when to go ahead or which turns to take. God's timing is right for you. Be confident in the knowledge that God will point out what you need to know along the way. If you can wait, you will soar.

wait

Teach us, O Lord, the disciplines of patience, for to wait is often harder than to work.

Peter Marshall

≫ In every delay this week, from traffic jams to work delays, ask God what he wants to teach you through your patience.

#88

Bind Up Bitterness

Put away from you all bitterness and wrath and anger and wrangling and slander, together with all malice.

Ephesians 4:31 NRSV

bind up

Is bitterness keeping you from finding and fulfilling God's purpose in your life? You have the power to get rid of bitterness and at the same time experience joy. When you have an unburdened heart, you give God a fertile ground in which to work.

People who caused you pain at some time may be long gone, and yet that pain has stayed in your heart as bitterness. But you can decide to let go of that bitterness. Ask God to unblock your heart. He will give you a fresh start, and you will be free to pursue the plans he has for you.

≫ Ask God to reveal any unresolved anger or bitter feelings you have, and ask God to help you get rid of them for good. Write your feelings on paper, and safely and symbolically burn them.

#89

Go Fishing

Fishing entails relaxing in the sun, preparing the tools you have, casting them out, and waiting expectantly for something good to happen. Fishing is a lot like God's purpose for you. He wants you to put the right tools in your kit, prepare your line, relax in him and the warmth of his embrace, and wait expectantly for the blessings that will come.

Jesus often went fishing with his disciples, but fish were not really what Jesus was after. He desired hearts and lives ready to prepare themselves and wait expectantly for a return. Find your purpose by getting your kit ready, and go fish.

> *If people concentrated on the really important things in life, there'd be a shortage of fishing poles.*
>
> Doug Larson

>> Read all the stories in the Gospels that involve fish. Then think about the ways you can add tools to your kit that will help you fulfill your purpose.

#90

Watch Others Work

> *Do you see a man diligent and skillful in his business? He will stand before kings; he will not stand before obscure men.*
>
> Proverbs 22:29 AMP

watch

People learn best by observing how someone else does something before trying it themselves. Experience, knowledge, ability, and strategies combine to do a job well. Watching someone else complete a task allows you to observe discipline and diligence in action so that you can apply the same techniques.

Build relationships by watching the efforts of those around you. Ask God to illuminate your role while you learn from the way others carry out their duties. You can appreciate their efforts while sharpening your own skills, and you can put the intellect God gave you to work for his glory.

≫ Ask a friend if you can watch closely as he goes about a specific task. See if you can learn something new, and use the opportunity to connect.

#91

Stand in the Gap

When you demonstrate faith, hope, and love to others during the times when they face a crisis, you fulfill God's purpose for your life by standing in the gap for them, especially if they do not have a relationship with God.

In that situation, you can seek God's purpose for you by praying for them, walking alongside them, and easing their burden in any way you can. When life's storms come and create a flood of emotions and difficulties for someone you know, you can stand in the gap for them, acting as the extension of the comforting hand of God.

stand

> *We must support one another, console one another, mutually help, counsel, and advise.*
>
> Thomas à Kempis

>> Share a meal with a friend who needs someone to stand in the gap. Fulfill God's purpose for your life by praying and helping him or her stand strong.

#92

Count Your Blessings

> *You will eat the fruit of your labor; blessings and prosperity will be yours.*
>
> Psalm 128:2 NIV

count

How often do you sit down and remember to count your blessings? Adding up all the good things in life takes more work than complaining, but it is very useful and enlightening. By taking stock of all God's blessings, you quickly remember how blessed you are just to be God's beloved creation, which leads to a deeper relationship with him.

God longs for you to appreciate his goodness to you. With the right heart attitude and the right words coming out of your mouth, remembering and counting your blessings will be a cinch. Observe the patterns of your blessings to discern God's direction for your life.

>> Cut thirty strips of construction paper an inch wide and four inches long. Write something good in your life on each strip, one for every day of the month. Make a paper chain of blessings to serve as a reminder.

#93

Pursue Passion

What is your passion? What makes you so excited, so keen, and so filled with joy and life that you can hardly keep your feet on the ground? Remember the passionate interests that you had when you were young? Find time to pursue those passions once again.

Develop your natural leanings and inclinations, the things that fill you with a sense of peace and satisfaction every time you put them to work. Do you love to draw? Draw with everything you have. Do you love to manipulate numbers? Calculate with enthusiasm. Instill excitement into what you do. God can use your fervor.

passion

> *I can't imagine a person becoming a success who doesn't give this game of life everything he's got.*
>
> Walter Cronkite

>> Discover what engages your passion. Take an aptitude test that allows you to check off what you like to do and that suggests professions and activities you might enjoy.

#94

Resurrect Him Daily

> *Declared to be the Son of God with power according to the Spirit of holiness, by the resurrection from the dead.*
>
> Romans 1:4 NKJV

resurrect

Seeking God's purpose for your life is a daily activity. Like waking, showering, dressing, eating breakfast, and brushing your teeth in the morning, developing a deep friendship with God takes repeated and daily efforts. It's never finished. Make a decision to connect with God, stay close to him, and be receptive to his leadership.

When you talk to God and follow him each day, your walk in faith becomes a natural and loved part of your life. You understand and appreciate Jesus' resurrection and know that he is alive and working vibrantly in your life. Resurrect him daily, and know true friendship with God.

≫ Spend time today resurrecting your relationship with God. Thank him for his resurrection power that can work in your life.

#95

Get on Your Knees

Occasionally you probably find yourself praying in some funny places. You may talk to God in your car, in your bed, at the dinner table, or behind your desk. All those places are fine, but there is also something important about getting on your knees.

Those who present themselves before royalty drop to their knees. It's a sign of humility, reverence, and an understanding of your position compared to the one on the throne. When you humble yourself before God, you open yourself to him and show him you are ready for him to use you to accomplish his great works.

knees

I have been driven many times to my knees by the overwhelming conviction that I had nowhere else to go.

Abraham Lincoln

≫ Spend time praying on your knees today, assuming a position of humbleness and telling God you are ready to be used for his purpose.

give

101 ways to

apply

memorize

breathe

consider

find God's purpose for your life

encourage

evaluate

wait

#96
Run the Race

> *You were running a good race. Who stopped you from following the true way?*
>
> Galatians 5:7 NCV

run

Life is a marathon, with roadblocks and hills to overcome along the way. God's purpose for you may be simply to run the race of life without giving up. Face the tough stretches and the easy strides with equal effort expended, and look to him for your direction.

In your daily life, keep your eyes on the finish line. God will provide grace and mercy along the journey when you begin to tire. He will refresh your soul, and through the Bible he will provide nourishment for you until you finish and receive the prize of eternity spent with him in heaven.

≫ Draw an oval "racetrack" in your prayer journal. Pencil in a finish line, and use the illustration to remind you to ask for God's help in getting closer to the finish line.

#97

Ask for Answers

If you seek to find God's purpose for your life, you should perfect the art of asking him questions. By inquiring of God what he wants you to do and how he wants you to do it, you give God the opportunity to help you take the right course of action. Seek to understand and to know your job. Ask him all five *W*s—who, what, when, where, why—and the *H*—how.

When you get your answers, pay attention to them and act on them. Once you ask, listen. Once you hear, act. Then you will hear God tell you, *Well done*.

ask

> *To ask well is to know much.*
>
> African Proverb

>> As you go about your week, write down a list of questions that you need to bring to God for his guidance. In your prayer time, ask your questions and ask him to help you listen for his answers.

#98

Let Him Have It

> *Cast all your anxiety on him because he cares for you.*
>
> 1 Peter 5:7 NIV

have it

Let God have all of you. All you are and all you experience and all you feel. Give God your joy, your fears, your love, and your pain. Get close to him, stay close to him, and give him all you are.

Give God all of you, every inch and fiber of your being. Give him your marriage, your friends, your children, and your coworkers. Give him your boss, your job, your abilities, and your household duties. You find his purpose when you surrender it all to him, recognizing that it is all his anyway, because he gave it to you.

≫ Gather pictures of your family and friends and use them in your prayer time today. Pray over them, and let God have your relationship with each one.

#99

Create a New Habit

By focusing your efforts on the positive, negative traits can fall away. For example, those who struggle to quit overeating may find success by drinking more water. Rather than depriving themselves of the food, they add water, thereby alleviating the bad habit by focusing on something good.

Finding God's purpose for your life means taking time to make good habits. Planning time for Bible study, taking good care of your body, and making sure you love are all good habits that help you fulfill your purpose. Instead of trying to quit negative habits, how about acquiring new, positive ones?

habit

It takes time for the fires to burn. It takes time for God to draw near and for us to know that He is there. It takes time to assimilate His truth. You ask me, How much time? I do not know. I know it means time enough to forget time.

John Mott

>> Develop a positive habit—reading your Bible, practicing an instrument for fifteen minutes, drinking more water, exercising—daily for six weeks. By then, your new habit should be firmly yours.

#100

Face Forward

> *Not that I have already attained, or am already perfected; but I press on, that I may lay hold of that for which Christ Jesus has also laid hold of me.*
>
> Philippians 3:12
> NKJV

forward

Discovering God's purpose for your life requires facing forward most of the time. In the race of life, you need to face the finish line and head toward it. Glancing behind gives good perspective, but you need to turn back around and face the front in order to make progress and fulfill your purpose.

Likewise, bringing lessons from the past to the present prepares you for the future; but living in the past prevents you from forging ahead. It's time to turn around and face forward. Thank God for the blessings of the past, and get ready to head into a fruitful future.

>> Think about how difficult it would be to fulfill God's purpose for you if you had to do everything backward. Ask God to help you let go of looking behind and instead face forward.

#101

Start Right Now

On your mark, get set, go! Remember how your heart would pound and the palms of your hands would sweat whenever you lined up for a race in physical education class, or whenever you stepped up to bat on the baseball team? The rush of adrenaline would propel you forward as soon as the signal to begin was given.

That's the way to approach your purpose in life, with heart pounding and feet ready to start pumping all the way to the finish line. Stumbling blocks will appear; trials will come. Your job is to stay focused on the tasks ahead and keep going. Ready? Go!

now

> *Every new day begins with possibilities.*
> Ronald Reagan

>> Map out your strategy for finding God's purpose for your life by listing your short-term and long-term goals for your mental, emotional, spiritual, and physical health.

I try to avoid looking forward or backward,
and try to keep looking upward.

Charlotte Brontë